AF408909

The Love: A Collection of Teenage Poems

AC Knight

Published by AC Knight, 2022.

While every precaution has been taken in the preparation of this book, the publisher assumes no responsibility for errors or omissions, or for damages resulting from the use of the information contained herein.

THE LOVE: A COLLECTION OF TEENAGE POEMS

First edition. November 20, 2022.

Copyright © 2022 AC Knight.

ISBN: 979-8215977682

Written by AC Knight.

For Jaboris.

The Love...

Young love is beautiful. It's make you want to write corny poetry for and to your muse. Do you remember the magic of your first love? Maybe a poem or two will spark your memory.

My Sweetest

I think of heaven when you're in my arms,
Everyone and everything matter's no more,
Looking in your brown eyes, nothing can go wrong,
My heart is what you've restored.
You're my Sweetest...
We were made for each other,
Lover to Lover.
I begin a sentence,
and the words you manage to finish.
You're my Sweetest...
My heart listens to every word you say,
I know those words aren't lies from you,
They are the promises and future of today,
Without them, I wouldn't know what to do.
You're my Sweetest...
My love for you shall remain everlasting,
like the image from an unforgettable painting.
My love for you shall remain so strong,
like the melody to an unforgettable wedding song.
You're my Sweetest...
You are the reason for my new-found hope,
I adore you.
I used to think love was a cruel joke,
but with you, I realize it's something deep and true.
You're my Sweetest...
It doesn't matter what people have said,
All their jealous conversation goes over my head.

You're like the sweetest poem I've ever read,
and you, my love, I will never forget.
You're my Sweetest...

<u>The Negro I desire</u>
to the negro I desire, I admire,
Whip it out, stick it in, I swear I'll never betray you for a white man
I Had My First taste of Chocolate at the age of 13 and ever since I've
been A feen.
African kings bring out my utmost self esteem
I'm addicted to the confidence
it's by no coincidence
You hold a power untouched
That's why they try to eliminate you from existence
It's true what they say about black men, egos so well endowed,
can you blame them for being jealous?
I admire your abilities to draw me in with your intelligence
Yet maintaining a masculine elegance
It's that certain level sexy
That makes your presence a necessity
An Adonis in the Greek sense
You must be of God-like descendant
Every woman falls to your knees
to obey, I surrender every inch of my female organs,
In a sad to attempt to persuade you to adore them,
Whip it out, stick it in, you have my word, I will never resort to white
men
It would be the ultimate sin.
To the negro, I desire, oh yes, I do admire.

<u>Forbidden Fruit</u>
Forbidden fruit, apple of my eye
A peach so sweet, a bite I can't deny
Every time we touch, I feel an eruption of volcanos and such
You are the reason Adam couldn't resist eve
You're like that taste of wine, so sweet and its fine
You're like the antivenom meant to save my life
A kiss from you is like falling off a cliff and hoping to fly
I'm under a voodoo spell when we connect
You cause all my sailing ships to wreck
It's something more than sex
I might need to be rehabilitated,
you're like my favorite drug, we're so well acquainted
You're like the ex that wasn't supposed to get that 2nd, 3rd,4th chance
You're so tricky and you know it, but for some strange reason I love it
I feen for it, I relish in it,
Damn...I ain't shit.
Oh well, I wanna take a bite of your tainted apple,
I'll take an entire mouth full
Forbidden fruit, apple of my eye
Like the peach I'm dying to try...

<u>Mushy</u>
At night I lay restless to the echoes of my every thought
It seems like I'm still fighting battles I've already fought
Going toe to toe with demons I thought I let go
They're trying to come back-to-back
Like biblical plagues
I light up my marijuana trees
And spread
I spread the smoke through my conscious like spiritual sage
I used to be out of control making decisions with such carelessness
Thinking I was flawless
How deep was my arrogance?
I'm selfish, the kind that only serves in my best interest
I'm tired of this, fighting the continuous battles to keep other people
feelings in perspective
I made a mistake thinking I'm the shit
Taking all your efforts for granted
yet you waited so patient for me to grow out of my immature ways
I'm hell bent on having your kids one of these days
I've grown so happy, gladly, and frankly you're surely the only one for me
please forgive me if I'm being mushy
But I'm giving myself to you just as you have given yourself to me

<u>They'll never understand</u>

They'll never understand how deep our love is, even when I hate you, I love you, you are the moon to my stars, the guide to my vision that allows me to see far

They'll never understand that our heart beats are in sink,

Our thoughts run together, so deep, I think it, you say it, I dream it, you believe it

They'll never understand that when you bleed, I feel it, your pain is just as much as mine, when I cry, you die

When I smile, you fly

They'll never understand that when our hands and body intertwine, they fit perfectly,

every kiss we share feels like the first time, as the years go by, we've aged so well to together like two bottles of fine wine

They'll never understand I was under your spell from the very first moment I laid eyes on you,

from that moment I knew, love could be something true, I've never been a true believer, but every moment with you makes my heartless demeanor grow weaker.

They don't understand from the outside looking in, we look so perfect but there are moments when we pretend, but no matter what I'm with you until the end.

They simply don't understand that you are mine and I am yours, and it will be that way until the world is no more.

<u>My Heart Sings</u>
It's been a long time since I've had my head so high in the sky
The question of why never crosses my mind.
When I think of you, I instantly smile
And like I said it's been a hell of a while.
You make me feel different though,
You came just in time to renew my hope,
In this potential thing called "love",
I swear it's as if God sent you from above.
You're the answer to all my questions,
The reason good things start to happen,
You're the prince in all the story books,
And I swear I've never been so hooked.
We can talk until the sun sets and rises,
You tell all your secrets so there are no bad surprises.
I tell you my thoughts as you listen,
I swear, you've finally released me from my dark prison.
Thinking of you is all I ever do
You're the person in my life that's new,
But it seems like I've known you forever
I know you're the one to make my future better.
You're wiser than any teacher,
Humbler than any preacher.
You have the looks of a movie star,
But in my eyes, you're light shines brighter than any star.
It's hard for me sometimes to put it in words
And even harder when I want to use verbs
But I write the way I'm feeling
I hope this poem is the utmost revealing.
I've found the sweetest man on this earth
And I'm pretty sure he appreciated me for all I'm worth.
I couldn't have imagined you in my wildest dreams

You're my reality that's why my heart sings.

<u>Me to see</u>
My sweetest dreams are made of the simplest moments sharing savory
kisses so succulent from your lips.
I often wonder wishes so whimsical it makes me ponder how real this is.
It's not often I question to my knowledge, the power of knowing and
not knocking the true existence of love.
I found a formula so forceful that it has all my focus, forcing me to take
it all in, I hope you've noticed.
An absolute terror I used to be, asserting myself so recklessly,
Absorbing the harshness of the streets, when all I had to do was open
my eyes, there you were for me to see.
There you were for me to see...
There you were for me to see.

<u>A Simple</u>

A kiss so soft so gentle,
A kiss so powerful to satisfy my mental.
A touch so warm and full of passion
A touch is all I wish to happen
A look so mesmerizing and compelling
A look so many words worth telling
A feeling of only being in heaven
A simple feeling of only your love I am craving.

<u>How Do I Perfect</u>
Give me a minute to think of what I want to say
I'm sorry but I'm at a loss of words almost every day...
Your beauty, no, the handsomeness you possess
Is fluttering my every thought and leaving me under duress
I can admire you from a distance
Because every day I am astonished by your magnificent existence
I... can't.. think...
Provide for me with the words to speak
Because the very sight of you makes me weak
Provide me with the courage
To control my uncontrollable urges
Give me a second...
To perfect this love method...

<u>One Number</u>
We could be like Melanie and Derwin without all the drama.
I'll scoop you up and take you home to meet my mama.
Maybe you can be my boo, but first I need your number.
It's true, we could be like Obama and Michelle, you'll be my presidential lover.
We could be like Jay-z and Beyonce, virtually music royalty.
We could be like an unknown celebrity couple,
you know, the one truly in love that the paparazzi can't bother.
We could be that unforgettable couple in movie made for romantic luster.
We could be that type of romance that only exist in a book.
I'll be your Bella you'll be my Edward, together we'll sit watching that magnificent eclipse.
We could be like Q and Monica, without the years of secretly wanting each other.
We could be some type of unorthodox fairy tale, be my Shrek, I'll be your Fiona, hell.
We could be the most famous of all couples, my favorite of all time,
the Romeo and Juliette of today without all the dying.
Take me while I'm still in my prime,
Take me while I haven't given up on trying.
We could be all we can be in any shape or wonder,
But first as I said, I need your number.

<u>*Speak to me, baby*</u>
I need the comfort of your conversation,
Talk to me for hours without hesitation.
Tell all the stories in your heart,
Tell all of them right from the start.
I can listen to your laughter,
Knowing what makes you happy is what I'm after.
Open up to me in ways you've never done before,
Put everything good and bad out on the floor.
Tell me your fears,
Tell me the first time you were brought to tears.
Tell me your secrets,
I swear in my diary is where I'll keep them.
Listen to my tales,
The stories of my triumphs and personal hell's.
Listen as I slowly break the barrier from around my heart
Tear down the bricks and make then into rocks
Take the rocks and throw them away
Steal my heart and claim it for the day
Tell me I am your one and only African queen
I'll tell you you're the king of my dreams.
Let me know your little secret plots
I'll tell you the few romantic gestures I've got.
I can talk to you until I there's no breath in my body,
Because that's how special you're becoming to me.
Give me your conversation,
Talk to me about everything with no hesitation.

<u>To my Friend</u>
Now you of all people know,
I've never been the type to fall in love
But boy you just might change that.
I can't get enough of your precious hugs
Or the way you brush my hair back
You tell me how special I am,
I believe it when it comes from you,
I think to myself you should be my man
Because only to you I'll be true.
I was so blinded with them other dudes
But you kept me intact, giving me advice.
You probably knew one day it'll be you I choose
I'm laughing because baby boy you might be right
Damn, it's crazy...
You know, how sometimes friends become lovers
At the same time it feels amazing
Knowing that you are the boy who is like no other.
I'm sitting right here typing this poem about you
Knowing that you'll probably read it
I'm laughing again because when you do
You'll know that everything I feel for you couldn't possibly fit
in poem or on this computer
So to my dear friend to whom I wrote this about
I laugh more because you know who you are

<u>"Love"</u>
Deeply feeling this thing called "love" is
strange.
Am I going insane or am I temporally
deranged?
No doubt, the heart will sometimes change,
But I guess my love for you will always be the

same.
I've never felt so deeply, this "love" thing
before.
You must really mean something to me.
At times I don't want to feel this way for
you,
Because I know some of the things guys
do
When a girl feels the way I do for you.
Deeply feeling this thing called "love" is not
my thing.
But I feel it,
And I feel it for you.

<u>To the Sweetest Guy I Know</u>
To the sweetest guy I know,
this is my love letter that
I think you should read.
We've known each other for
a while now and in all
that time, you've always
made me smile.
In the past I've done you wrong,
but we've managed to keep singing
that same old love song.
Thinking about you is the highest of my joys,
talking to you means there's no other noise
You are my sunshine at night
With you, I know everything is going to be alright.
I don't ever want to think about us not being together.
We will be in love forever.
To the sweetest guy I know
this is my love letter,

To sum it all up, I just
want to say I love you.
You'll be forever my boo.

Basketball & Love
The bouncing of the heart plus the ball
equals love and basketball.
The shooting and scoring plus
the kissing and hugging equals basketball
and love.
The free throws missed are the heartaches
involved in this, love and basketball.
In the end, who will win? Love or Pain?
We'll never know until we play the game
of Basketball and Love.

Being with You

Talking to you brings me the most joys,
Being with you is the peak of my happiness.
When I say I love you, I mean it.
It isn't a lie or a misleading trick.
You are my life and my sunshine at night.
You are the dreams I dream in my sleep.
Talking to you is never enough.
Every African queen needs a king,
will you be my king?
You and I are a good thing.
We belong together like peaches and cream.
Being without you would drive me insane.
I don't how many times I can say it,
But I simply love being with you...

I Love You

There are no ways to express how I feel for you.
I can't explain but I love you.
You are my world, you are my life.
You give me peace when I don't feel right.
I can't explain but I love you.
When we get married, I will cherish and love you
for the rest of my life.
Baby, I am your wife.
I can't explain but I love you.
There is really no way I can show the way I feel for you
All I can say is... I love you.

<u>Wanting You</u>
Wanting you is like a drug when I need it
I must have your love.
To feel your heartbeat as I lay on
your chest is my fantasy more or less.
My heart yearns for your tender kiss,
with that I might add, is my first wish.
Wanting you there is no day, evening,
or night,
There is only the chance
that we might...
Needing you feels so good,
Wanting you is understood,
Having you I wish I could.

<u>To Him</u>
There's this guy
who loves me just
as much as I love him
But I already have an
husband.
He makes me feel
like the world is in
my hands and his
powerful gaze puts me
in a trance.
He sits and waits
but what I really need is for
him to take my other
man's place.
To him I would give my all to
If he just realizes what he has

to do.

<u>Desire</u>
Can you feel my desire?
Can you sense it floating around me?
Can you see the fire in my eyes?
Can you hear my heart pounding?
Can you feel the vibrations humming?
Desire.
Can you feel it now?
Can you feel my desire?
<u>Something Special</u>
Trying to think of something special
to write.
I don't know why but my hearts seems to
takes flight
When I'm looking into my baby's eyes.
The way I feel for him is driving me crazy!
I don't know how to put it in words
And that's something that is absurd.
I'm lost in him.
I'm an inmate in his prison,
of love that is.
I consider you the blessing
I've been asking for,
the perfect guy I didn't
believe existed anymore.
But you do, you do.
I find it funny I
stumbled upon you.
My dream, no, my reality is
when I'm with you.
You make my rainy days
sunny again,

You keep it real wit me,
I don't have to pretend.
You're different,
And I'm loving every second
Of your positive presence.
It's making a difference in my life,
Being with you, I want to do right.
I'm not living in the past anymore
because my present is something I adore,
your loveliness is hard to ignore

<u>One love to give</u>
I've only got one heart to live with,
And I've only got one brain to think with.
I've got two eyes to see,
And I've got too lungs to breathe.
I've got one heart to give,
And only one time to fix it if it breaks.
I've got nothing but love in my soul,
And sometimes it's so hard to control.
I've got people who love me dearly,
I've got those who fear me.
I've got sunshine on a cloudy day,
And I've got no real bills to pay.
I've got the love of my true friends,
And I've got the love of my only man.
I've got God in my spirit,
And I don't care if you don't believe it.
I've got one love to give,

<u>My Angel</u>
The One sent from the heavens above.
My angel,
The one sent to bring me eternal love.
My angel,
The one sent to rescue me from my personal hell.
My angel,
The one to save me from my personal jail.
My angel,
The one with the heavenly brown eyes.
My angel,
The one who's body never lies.
My angel,
The one with those heavenly lips.
My angel,
The one with the most passionate kiss.
My angel,
The one I met when I was lost.
My angel,
The one who will be there for me at every cost.
My angel,
The one who keeps me sane.
My angel,
The one who tells me the world is not to blame.
My angel,
The one that takes my breath away.
My angel,
The one I live for every day.
My angel,
The one the lord assigned to me.
My angel,
With you my heart will always be.

<u>Flaws and I</u>
Emotional, Angry, Panicky,
Selfish, Apathetic, Overdramatic,
Boring, Lazy, Indifferent, Thoughtless,
Envious, indecisive, Stubborn, Cruel,
Impatient, Sarcastic, Nonchalant, Basket Case.
With all that I am, you're stuck with me.
It would be simple to leave,
Because loving me won't be easy,
And you're crazy to take on such a challenge,
But you're not like the others, you're not average.
I guess I can appreciate the flaws I have
Hoping they won't last.
I guess I'll have to love my flaws and I.

<u>All I Need</u>
Floating in a pool of ecstasy
Realizing that all I need is you next to me.
What's my desire?
Anything you can do to take me higher.
What's my fantasy?
For you to set my body free.
Floating in a pool of ecstasy
Realizing all I need is you next to me.
How can you make me happy?
Tell me every day that you're lucky.
How can you keep me satisfied?
Showing me you're willing to admit you tried.
Floating in a pool of ecstasy
Realizing that all I need is you next to me.
All I need is you next to me...
All I need is you next to me...

If You Only Knew
Something about you makes me smile,
I always get lost thinking about you,
If only you knew...
My feelings are everywhere when it comes to you,
I want to tell you something, but I can't,
If only you knew...
I am a hopeless romantic.
Yes, I wrote this poem about you,
I am obsessed with you,

if only you knew,

How much I truly like you.
If only you knew, I'd try to get away
From everything just to be with you,
if only you knew...

When Will I Find You?
When will I find that person that is true and mine?
When will I find that person that is true and mine?
Will he fall into my arms or will I fall into his?
When will I have the right to be called Mrs.?
Is that person here right in front of me?
Or will I have to search for my husband to be?
When will I find that person?
If I find him will things worsen?
Am I destined to be alone?
No, I'm not, so I'll keep singing my love songs.

Chain Reaction of Cupid
Wondering what to do to get you.

I wonder why I die every time you look.
You've got me caught on your hook.
Are you going to be my boo?
Or do you want me to be just for you?
I can't deny I am in love,
Cupid, will you please shoot that arrow from above.
Please don't let him hang with his crew,
And leave me to stand like a fool,
Please don't hold that arrow back,
Turn his head to me,
Let me be cool,
This is not an act,
Together we can be.

<u>Just Nervous</u>
It's in the corner of my eye
I see you pass me by.
The butterflies float in my stomach,
I can't control it.
I blush when you brush by me
And every time that happens I plea,
That your eyes wonder towards me
Just nervous when I get around you.
I can't seem to figure out what to do.
I'm nervous, I'm nervous,
and I can't help it when I see you.

<u>Butterflies</u>
What is this feeling I feel that I can't describe
but is real?
Who is this person that has my heart racing
every time I approach him?
He gives me butterflies...

Butterflies that have me stuck,
I can't get away from them.
I'm sure he gets them too, making him
feel all funny inside...
We will continue to have these feelings for each other...
These butterflies...

Chain Reaction of Cupid Part 2
Together we'll be,
You and me.
If you look you'll see,
I'm for you and you're for me.
We're two of a kind.
I've got your back, you've got mine.
Thank you Cupid, for your reaction,
You came through for my satisfaction.
I wasn't left there like a fool,
He took my hand, it was heaven sent,
I remained still, I remained cool.
Together we are one.
One kiss wouldn't be going too far.

My Love Letter
You are something special to me,
I can see we were meant to be.
The way we hold hands trying our
Best to be the best of friends.
My love for you is so simple,
Your feelings for me are gentle.
No words or physical things can be compared to you,
From the first day I saw you, I knew,
You were going to be something special,
And this is my love letter to you.

Hard 2 Get

Why don't you just stop playing so hard to get?
Is it because I misrepresent myself to you?
Is it because my Ex might ruin our progress?
Or is it that you don't want to take a chance?
My heart is only for you,
But that's not what you know.
You know it was cute for a while,
The way you passed by me and smiled,
Without so much as a word,
But if you haven't heard
I don't have a lifetime to wait
What's it going to be?
Will you be mine or a waste of time?
Too good to let true love shine for yourself
I just want you to know,
I'm here, ready and trying,
But baby, you're playing too hard to get.

Don't Quit

He is going to be mine,
I don't care who he belongs now,
I want him back in my life,
I need him like an addict needs drugs,
I need him like water,
He is something I try to refuse, but can't
I'm going to get him back
the other girls are going to have to cope with that.
Whether it be flirting, smiling, touching, or talking,
We're getting back together,
Screw whoever doubts us.
I won't quit until he is the one I'm with.

<u>You</u>
It is you I want and need
Excuse my greed,
Your look, your smile
Drives me wild,
I can't help it,
I'm selfish.
You're the one
who makes me feel good.
You're the one I would
spend forever with if I could.
Maybe it's because I love you,
(Yea this is true)
I don't know how you feel,
Are you immature or real?
I don't know how to say it,
But I'm sure you are who you are,
I love you no matter what you do,
Don't ever stop being you.

<u>A Gift from A Sagittarius</u>
I fell in love with a Sagittarius,
He seemed to be serious,
Like myself...
Lips so luscious,
He seemed to be delicious,
Like myself...
We flipped sides like Gemini's,
It came to be no surprise,
Like ourselves...
My gift from a Sagittarius to another,
Is like no other,

I offer myself...
I fell in love with a Sagittarius
Who left me speechless

<u>*Dangerous, but love*</u>
I am in danger because I am in love,
But he has no love.
I sit and wait, and wait, and wait,
For our first date.
Wait, I forget...he already has a mate.
I wonder why sometimes you'd fight for love
You push and shove for that "L" word.
It's dangerous but it's love, my love.

<u>*Just One*</u>
You want to, just one kiss,
I want to see if you're right for me.
I know we're friends, but I feel
There's something more,
I know you see how we sit and adore
Each other's presence,
The way we look in each other's eyes
I've noticed.
I promise nothing will change,
It will all be the same,.
I know it's not normal for friends to do this,
Date, hold hands, and kiss,
But I want to make sure
You're not the one to get away,
Just stay.
One kiss and I'll be on my way,
One kiss will conquer my unseen greed
I know you really want to.

I Think About

When I think about you I get lost in my thoughts,
My mind seems to explore the possibilities
that you and I will be.
When I dream I never want to wake up
Because in that world I have nothing but luck.
Shutting my eyes, I see your beautiful face,
It seems like no other image can take your place.
I get lost in you, I lose myself talking to you,
I can't really express how I feel other than to write it
And hope that you feel it.
Why do all my daydreams
somehow take a spin in your direction.
It's driving me crazy, but I like it.
I can't help but to think about your lips
Touching mine, your fingers rolling down
My spine, I guess I love to think about
You all the time in my hopeless mind.

I Love My Baby

I love my baby,
the way he holds me,
The way he touches me,
The way he feels for me.
I love my baby,
The way he laughs,
The way he talks,
The way he walks and smells.
I love my baby,
The way he looks,
The way he smiles,
The way he drives me wild.

I love my baby and the way he loves me.

<u>Prince Charming</u>
I found you, I finally found you,
The one I want to give my heart to.
My prince, the charming,
The man I've always been wanting for.
You came from nowhere on your stallion,
My heart pounding past a million,
I've been trapped in a tower of loneliness,
With many thoughts of escaping it.
You found me, you finally found me,
My handsome prince charming.

<u>Heartbeat</u>
Thump, bump, thump, bump
I hear as I lay my ear across your chest.
Thump, bump, thump, bump
You hear as you lay across my breast.
They beat as one,
They beat steady like a drum.
Thump, bump, thump, bump
It goes as I anticipate your next touch.
Thump, bump, thump, bump
To hear it is an absolute must.
Your heartbeat gives me everlasting love.

<u>A New Love</u>
Time for you to sweep me off my feet
Time to take me out on a date to a fancy restaurant to eat
Time for you to tell me I'm your world
Time for you to make me feel like a special girl
Time for you to look me deeply in my eyes
Time to make me feel like you're not like other guys

Time to have a love and basketball romance
Time to dream about our wedding in France
Time for you to be Aladdin and for me to be Jasmine
Time for our love, like an album, to go platinum
Time to start an infectiously reckless but beautiful trend
Time for me to fall hopelessly in love again...

<u>*And I'll Be*</u>
And I'll be your friend...
The one you will call on for the smallest advice,
The one you can cry to when all is not right,
The one you can count on in a fight,
The shoulder you can lean on in despair,
The one who will always be there,
The one who will tell you when you've
done something stupid,
The one you can laugh with for no apparent reason,
The one to call you names and tease,
The one who will fight you with ease,
The one you will always trust and believe,
The one you'll give your last dollar,
The one who will get you out of trouble,
The one who will care when no else does,
The one who will give unconditional love.
Yeah...I'll be your Friend.
And I'll be your lover...
The one who will stare deeply in your eyes
wondering what's running through your mind,
The one who will face every mountain there is to climb,
for you...
The one who's feelings will never be new,
The one who's arms will hold you in your weakest moment,
The one who will whisper sweet nothings in your ear,
The one who's love will never disappear,
The one who will argue with you for no apparent reason,
The one who will challenge you to be a better man every season,
The one who will prove anything in your name,
The one who will to take the blame,
The one who will listen when you're in pain,

The one who will make your days brighter,
The one who will be your unconditional lover.
Yeah...I'll be your Lover.
And I'll be...Whatever you want me to be...
As long as I'm with you...I'll be...

<u>Ultimate Love</u>
Call me baby, call me your ultimate love.
Call me the women of your dreams
the women sent from above.
Call me your African goddess
Call me your favorite Hollywood actress.
Call me the women who can satisfy your every desire
Call me whatever you want, know that I'm not a liar.
Call me the women in the dirty magazines
Call me for all the physical love I bring.
Call me your favorite video game
Call me one and one the same.
Call me baby, call me your ultimate love.

<u>I'm Selfish (with you)</u>
I'm selfish when it comes to you
Can't help it when it comes down to you
I'm crazy when it comes down to you...with you.
Share you with someone else?
No, I don't think that's a possibility,
You're good for my health,
making my existence logical,
Me living by myself,
A thought so irrational,
Don't know what I'd do,
don't know what I'd do without you.
I'm selfish when it come to you,
Can't help it when it comes down to you,
I'm crazy when it comes down to you...with you,
Don't mind my jealousy,
I see those other girls looking,
They can't satisfy you like I do mentally,
Just make sure you let them know you're mine for the taking
Having a misunderstanding would end in something terribly mistaking,
Other women are going to send me in jail,
Because I don't know what I'd do,
Don't know what I'd do without you.
I'm selfish when it comes to you
Can't help it when it comes down to you
I'm a little crazy when comes down to you...with you.
<u>Building Blocks of Love</u>
I met ya, then I liked ya
I liked ya, then I crushed on ya
I crushed on ya, then I got tah know ya
I got tah know ya, then I started falling for ya.
I started falling for ya, then I fell in love wit cha....

I don't feel my love getting any weaker,
What strong foundation...

<u>Poem 2</u>

I'll always find my way back,
back to what matters the most,
the most amazing human being is you,
You...I lost you once, it won't happen again.
again, we fight and break up,
break up, in five minutes we make up,
make up is what we do because we are in love
love, a word I honestly don't understand the meaning of but I feel,
feel, feel like I need to be telling you that you're the only one that matters,
matters, does it matter that others are after,
after us because we're so perfectly imperfect,
imperfect we are as human beings, but the chase is worth it,
worth it is what you are to me,
to me is who you belong to,
to you, I will always find my way back to.

<u>Poem 1</u>

I only have eyes for you
I'm fascinated, almost fixated
unable to dim the heavenly glow
you've presented like the beginning of the rainbow
so wondrous, so spectacular
a rare vision, my eyes glued, attached to ya
I only see what god has allowed of me
a true testament to inner and outer beauty
my reality consists of your vanity
unfortunately, I become ever so weak
in a presence of someone resembling an African god
I've been mesmerized from the very start

us ever going in separate directions
would only lead to hopeless depression,
as I have stated before you are undoubtfully
my fixation and the owner of my admiration
thanking my lord above for such a magnificent
creation, my vision depends on your existence
without you, my eyes would be useless
If only you had the slightest clue
I only have eyes for you.

<u>I Only See Beauty</u>
How can I marvel at a beauty so unattainable?
Frozen in your presence, a feeling so unexplainable
The words are lost as I begin to express my admiration
A pause...causing my thoughts to enter a state of inhalation
Your eyes are my fixation
Your skin, so soft, so amazing
I take another step closer
To begin this conquest of love with a total stranger
My only concern is that I haven't fallen so quickly
I pray that I fall for your personality
Because beauty is only skin deep.

<u>Superhero Love</u>
If he is superman
I will never be his Lois lane
I'll be his wonder woman instead
Because we are equally the same
That damsel in distress bullshit is lame
I'll never be that dependent woman because
that shit is weak.
He loves how strong I am, how I challenge his wits
Sometimes he needs me to rescue him
I'll do it with a fight but at the same time no questions
I'm the shoulder he will lean on
He's the chest I can rest on
My superhuman strength will provide him with the relaxation he craves.
To become his equal, you must trust a man to fight with you the evil.
Every man needs a woman who makes him feel complete
Every woman needs a man who makes her feel complete
Superman can't always do it by himself,
No to worry, wonder woman is there to help.
I'll be his wonder woman,
I'll be his wonder woman,
His wonder woman is me
We'll fly away together to another galaxy...

Like Lauryn Said
Like Lauryn said the sweetest thing I've ever known
Was like a kiss on the collarbone
How I can stay up all night with you on the phone
No wonder my mind is so gone.
I don't ever have to hear your voice
To know living without me is not a choice
I don't have to sit right here and pretend
Because every moment I have with you
I hope occurs again
I wanna laugh with you until
I can't breathe
I wanna be forever the one that says
Bless you when you sneeze
I wanna be in the passenger side of
Your car just to let the hoes looking in
Know they're not gonna get far.
For you I would break the law because being with
You must be illegal.
I want the judge to sentence me to a lifetime
Nuzzled peacefully in your arms
I'll be a convict in that prison behind bars
Like Lauryn said the soft caress of happiness
I want to take all your stress away with
a single touch,
In my fingers you will feel the root of all
my love
I'll message your upper and lower back
The work you do is hard so you
deserve only that.
I'll admit that you are king, not necessary is a ring
I am yours and you are mine.

Lauryn said it, but I've always known
That you were the sweetest thing.

Made For Each Other
Found someone better
Ready to do whatever
with me though any type of weather
he will treat me like a queen
he admires my high self esteem
Been friends for a while
even when I was running wild
One man's loss is another man's treasure
One girl doesn't hold his interest, another will do it better.
Opposites sometimes attract
It's the similarities that will keep us intact.
Waiting for someone that was right in my face
Patient, he was, never concerned about the race.
My heart is what he will cherish
With his heart I will no longer be careless.
A relationship I know I can be honest in
A relationship I'm certain will never end.
We know each other too well
Anyone trying to come between us will fail.
Hearts have been broken
Trust was stolen.
In the end I could always count on him
The rode ahead won't be easy
At the end of the day, I'll still need him as well as he needs me.

Heaven's Gates

I have been in love with you from the very moment we shared our first
kiss
Falling in love sooner was my only wish
I lay next to you at night thinking there is no other way to live
When I'm away from, my only thoughts are of your kiss

I'm amazed at how another human being could have such an effect on me
You aren't just my lover, but a part of me, connected to me, literally inside of me, my identity.
I know our hearts beat as one, but we are the only ones listening
I'll never feel the grasp of your love loosening from my soul,
I share in all honesty that you might be the one and only true love for me
They could write our love in history, but it will never be accurate
They know every fact, but they've never lived it
Our love is as sacred as the vow of the holiest of men, we can't fake it
But I know for a fact no one could ever relate
It is you, I now know my fate
I'm to forever to find comfort in your arms because they are like heavens gates

<u>Happy Anniversary</u>
What a man, what a man, your what I think of when I think of a man
How lucky am I to have you as my husband
The king of our future kingdom
I am your queen who will never commit treason
With God-like qualities, I admire you
The hard work, greatness is what you pursue
The provider, the protector, the privilege that is your presence
If I believed in prayer, you would be my ultimate blessing
True loves kiss from you was my first lesson
Not snatching you up sooner is my only confession
A fool to almost lose you as my most prized possession
A love that has continuously reached new states of progression
Into something like a flower blooming into adulthood
Like a wildfire my passion burns for your very touch
This isn't what the bible deems as lust but is in fact love.
I am in love with you, words I stand by the very moment I said I do
This is my poem of love, so happy anniversary to you.

FOR JABORIS

I dedicated this book to you because I've loved you since I was 19 years old. I know our love story has been complicated but it's a journey I wish to continue. You've inspired me in ways you can't even imagine. You've supported and believed in me through every phase of my life. I love you and wish to spend the rest of my days with you. My honeydip.

Love Alexis.

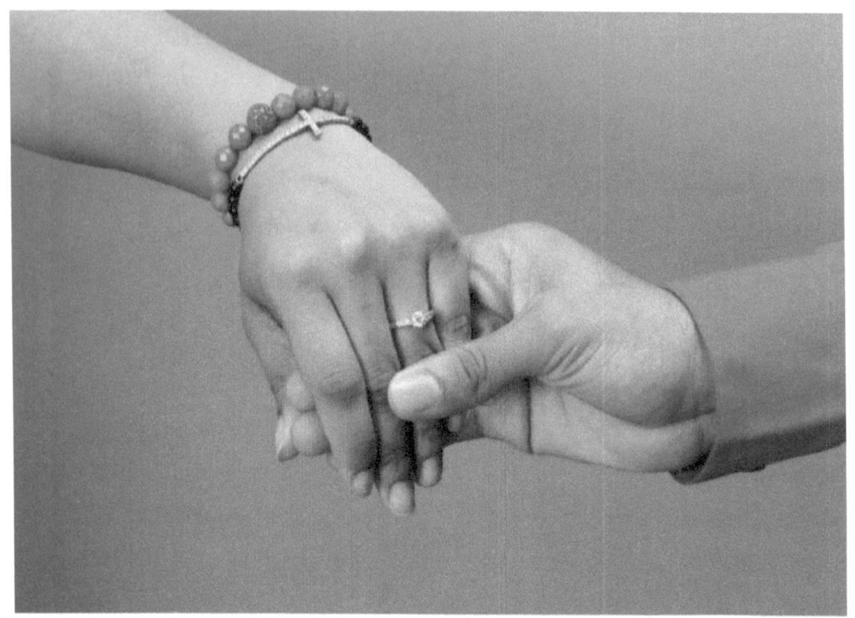

About the Author

AC Knight is a Chicago native who's also a United States Navy veteran. She is currently a student at Tidewater Community College pursuing her Associates Degree in General Studies with plans to transfer to a university to complete a Creative Writing Bachelor's degree.

Inspired by the late great Maya Angelou, she has always had a passion for writing with plans to release a series of novellas. She resides in Portsmouth, Virginia with her loving husband, daughter and two Siberian huskies